CW01472139

Original title:
Love's True Path

Author: Paul Pääsuke
ISBN HARDBACK: 978-9916-87-315-1
ISBN PAPERBACK: 978-9916-87-316-8
ISBN EBOOK: 978-9916-87-317-5

Beyond the Bridges of Time

Across the river, shadows play,
Whispers of the night, they sway.
Footprints echo on the shore,
To memories that we adore.

Stars above, they softly shine,
Marking moments, yours and mine.
Together we will chase the light,
Beyond the bridges, out of sight.

Weaving Dreams of Togetherness

In the loom of dusk, we meet,
Threads of laughter, warm and sweet.
Each stitch a wish, a hope embraced,
Together woven, time not wasted.

Colors blend in perfect tune,
Underneath the watchful moon.
Crafting futures, hand in hand,
Dreams like castles built on sand.

The Roads We Dare to Tread

Paths uncertain, wide and free,
Boundless tales that wait for thee.
With every step, we claim our ground,
In every turn, new joys abound.

Mountains high and valleys low,
Together we shall bravely go.
The journey calls, our hearts align,
In every heartbeat, you are mine.

Raindrops on a Shared Umbrella

Pattering softly on the sheet,
A symphony of hearts that meet.
Underneath the fabric's grace,
Finding warmth in each embrace.

The world fades into muted hues,
With every drop, our love renews.
Holding close, we brave the storm,
In shared shelter, we are warm.

Heartstrings in Cosmic Harmony

Beneath the stars, our whispers blend,
A symphony of hearts that never end.
In cosmic dance, we sway and twine,
Each pulse a note, your heart to mine.

Through nebulae, our dreams take flight,
In galaxies forged, we find our light.
With every breath, the universe sings,
In this vast space, our love takes wing.

The Unfolding Scroll of Us

Pages turn in the book of time,
Each line crafted, a wordless rhyme.
In ink of moments, our stories spill,
A tapestry woven with heart and will.

Chapter by chapter, we chart the course,
With laughter and tears, a binding force.
Through shadows cast and brightening dawn,
The scroll unfolds, our journey drawn.

Beyond the Horizon of Desire

Where dreams converge on the edge of night,
A canvas of hues, soft and bright.
With every heartbeat, the world expands,
Waves of longing that time commands.

Together we reach for the distant shore,
Where wishes dance and spirits soar.
Beyond the horizon, love's gentle fire,
A land where hopes bloom, beyond desire.

Through the Veil of Connected Souls

In twilight's glow, we find our thread,
A fabric of souls, in silence bred.
With eyes like mirrors, we dare to see,
The hidden depth of you and me.

Through veils that shimmer, we walk as one,
In unity's grace, our fears undone.
With every heartbeat, a story told,
Bound by a love that never gets old.

Stars That Cross Our Skies

Bright diamonds swirl in night,
They whisper secrets, soft and light.
Each twinkle tells a story old,
Of dreams and wishes, brave and bold.

In velvet darkness, they align,
Guiding hearts with paths divine.
A dance of lumens, fierce and free,
They shine for you, they shine for me.

Echoes of Sheltered Souls

Within the quiet, hearts take flight,
Echoing softly through the night.
Whispers linger, gently spun,
In hidden corners, love is won.

Sheltered voices, sweetly blend,
In a melody that knows no end.
Each note a promise, pure and clear,
A symphony for all to hear.

The Tides of Gentle Yearning

Waves of longing softly roll,
Caressing shores, they seek a goal.
Each crest a dream that curls and bends,
In the embrace where time suspends.

Salted breezes kiss the air,
Filling hearts with love and care.
In the rhythm, we find our way,
As tides of yearning guide the day.

When Two Hearts Converge

Two hearts collide, a spark ignites,
In this moment, pure delights.
Eyes meet like stars in perfect sync,
In silence shared, our thoughts entwink.

With every heartbeat, whispers flow,
A language only we would know.
Together we stand, strong and true,
When two hearts converge, love breaks through.

Under the Umbrella of Understanding

In the rain of doubt we stand,
Together beneath the spread hand.
Whispers of hope swirl around,
In the shelter, peace is found.

Hearts open wide, embrace the glow,
In the warmth, love starts to flow.
Through storms of hurt, we hold on tight,
With every challenge, shines our light.

A Dance of Stars Crossing

In the velvet night we twirl,
Dreams like glittering pearls do swirl.
Every glance a spark ignites,
In the cosmos, joy takes flight.

Constellations dance in sync,
Moments shared make hearts rethink.
As auroras kiss the sky,
In this dance, no need to fly.

The Secret Gardens of Affection

Hidden blooms in shadows grow,
Tender whispers, soft and slow.
In the silence, feelings weave,
A tapestry we both believe.

Every petal, a soft sigh,
Anchored deep, where secrets lie.
In this garden, shadows play,
Nurtured dreams lead us away.

The Echoing Footsteps of Two

On the path where silence speaks,
Footsteps echo, love it seeks.
With each step, our story grows,
In harmony, our essence flows.

Through the valleys, high and low,
Together, hand in hand, we go.
In the echoes, memories gleam,
A journey shared, a common dream.

The Dance of the Unseen Connection

In shadows where whispers softly bloom,
Two souls entwined, in silence they loom.
A glance exchanged, like a fleeting spark,
In the heart's deep well, they leave their mark.

Like stars that twinkle in the midnight sky,
They drift through dreams, their spirits fly.
A waltz of fate, unseen yet true,
In every breath, they find their view.

The world may fade, but bonds hold tight,
A dance of love in the pale moonlight.
With every step, the magic grows,
An embrace of souls that only they know.

In harmony's cradle, they find their place,
Two hearts in rhythm, a tender grace.
Through the unseen, they'll always stay,
In the dance of life, they find their way.

Trails of Resilient Hearts

In every stumble, a lesson learned,
Through winding paths, the fire burned.
With scars to show, but spirits bright,
They journey on, embracing light.

Mountains rise and valleys fall,
Yet resilient hearts, they stand tall.
Each step a song, a story to tell,
In unity strong, they break the spell.

Through storms and shadows, they navigate,
Finding hope in every fate.
With courage fierce, they face the winds,
On trails of love, the journey begins.

A tapestry woven with threads of gold,
Of dreams and wishes, brave and bold.
Together they walk, a rhythmic beat,
In the trails of life, they never retreat.

Serene Journeys of Togetherness

Together we walk, hand in hand,
Through fields of peace, so vast and grand.
With every step, we share our dreams,
Beneath the sun, by gentle streams.

In silence deep, our hearts align,
With whispers soft, like aged wine.
Each moment treasured, pure delight,
In every dawn, and every night.

Through valleys low and mountains high,
In laughter bright, we touch the sky.
Together we journey, side by side,
In love's embrace, we shall abide.

Whispers in the Heart

With quiet tones, the heart does speak,
In gentle sighs, it finds the meek.
A melody of love so true,
In whispers soft, it calls to you.

Beneath the stars, our secrets blend,
In every beat, a lover's friend.
The world fades out, it's just us two,
A sacred space where dreams come through.

In fleeting glances, warmth ignites,
Two shadows dance in moonlit nights.
With every touch, a silent vow,
In whispers soft, we live the now.

A Journey Through Unseen Roads

On paths unknown, we venture forth,
With hearts alight, we seek our worth.
Through winding trails and hidden bends,
The journey calls, where love transcends.

In shadows deep, we find our light,
With courage bold, we face the night.
With every step, our spirits soar,
Together we seek, forevermore.

In distant lands, where dreams unfold,
The stories whispered, yet untold.
With hands entwined, we'll face the day,
Through unseen roads, we find our way.

The Compass of Affection

In every glance, a guiding star,
With love as light, we travel far.
Through storms and calm, we hold the true,
Our hearts the compass, me and you.

With every touch, the world aligns,
In fleeting moments, joy shines bright.
Through rough terrain and gentle streams,
We chart our course, pursue our dreams.

In laughter's echo, we'll steer our ship,
With kindness deep, we'll let love slip.
Through life's vast sea, we navigate,
With hearts united, we celebrate.

Whispers of the Heart's Journey

Through valleys deep, where shadows play,
The whispers trace our steps each day.
With every beat, a tale unfolds,
In silent dreams, our love is bold.

Across the streams, the echoes flow,
In gentle winds, our stories grow.
With every tear, a bridge we build,
The heart's sweet song, forever thrilled.

In distant stars, our wishes gleam,
And in the night, we dance and beam.
A journey shared, we laugh and cry,
On wings of hope, we learn to fly.

The Compass of Affection

A needle points to where you are,
In every hug, a guiding star.
With every glance, it pulls us near,
In this vast world, you are my sphere.

Through storms we sail, with hearts aligned,
In every challenge, love defined.
Your laughter echoes, sweet as wine,
A compass true, our fates entwined.

With kindness sewn in every seam,
Together, weaving every dream.
A map of trust, of joy and grace,
In your embrace, I find my place.

When Souls Align

In quiet moments, eyes can meet,
A spark ignites, our hearts repeat.
Like constellations in the night,
Two souls converge, a wondrous sight.

With every breath, we learn to share,
In whispered words, we show we care.
Paths intertwine, like vines that climb,
In sacred dance, we lose all time.

The universe hums a gentle tune,
As two hearts beat in love's sweet boon.
In harmony, our spirits soar,
In love's embrace, forevermore.

Echoes of Unseen Bonds

In shadows cast, our spirits twine,
An unseen thread, a love divine.
Through thick and thin, we sense the call,
In silent whispers, we stand tall.

A glance exchanged, a knowing sigh,
In every step, you're by my side.
The echoes ring, a timeless song,
In the heart's language, we belong.

With every memory, light will bloom,
In depths of silence, love finds room.
Though worlds apart, our hearts combine,
In echoes soft, our souls align.

The Light That Guides Us Home

In the dark where shadows creep,
A flicker shines, a promise to keep.
Through twisting paths and winding roads,
A beacon glows, it lightens loads.

Whispers call from distant lands,
Guiding hearts with gentle hands.
Trust the light that leads the way,
It never falters, come what may.

Threads of Destiny Intertwined

In the loom of fate we meet,
Strings of chaos form a beat.
Each encounter, a subtle weave,
In shared moments, we believe.

Patterns change as seasons flow,
Stories merge, then gently go.
With every glance, a thread is spun,
In the tapestry, we are one.

In the Garden of Endless Possibilities

Petals whisper in the breeze,
Dreams take flight among the trees.
Colors dance in the morning light,
Each bloom a wish, pure and bright.

Paths unfold, both near and far,
Finding hope in every star.
Nature's song sings true and clear,
A world of wonders drawing near.

Sunsets Beyond the Cliffs of Time

Hues of amber stretch the sky,
As day bids evening a soft goodbye.
Waves below sing a lullaby,
To moments lost as hours fly.

Each sunset wraps the world in grace,
A fleeting glimpse, a warm embrace.
Beyond the cliffs, where dreams reside,
We find our strength, our hearts collide.

Ambling Through the Love-Laden Forest

In the cool shade, whispers sigh,
Leaves dance softly, as time flies by.
Branches weave a tapestry bright,
Embracing hearts in gentle light.

Paths entwined, hands held tight,
With every step, the world feels right.
Echoes of laughter fill the air,
In this forest, love we share.

In Step with the Heart's Whisper

Quiet moments, hearts align,
In the stillness, love's design.
Every heartbeat, soft and clear,
Guides us closer, drawing near.

With every breath, a secret vow,
In the present, here and now.
Listen closely, hear the sound,
Of our love, forever bound.

The Kaleidoscope of Shared Moments

Colors blend in vibrant hues,
Memories spin, each joy we choose.
In laughter and tears, we find our way,
A tapestry woven day by day.

Every glance, a story told,
In this dance, our hearts unfold.
Moments cherished, never lost,
In the fabric of love, we pay the cost.

The Bridge Crafted by Understanding

Across the stream, where shadows play,
A bridge unseen leads hearts to sway.
Crafted gently with whispered trust,
In the bond that is firm and just.

Footsteps echo on sturdy beams,
Linking souls, igniting dreams.
Together we stand, side by side,
On understanding, we will glide.

The Tapestry of Us

In the threads of laughter, we sew,
Woven dreams, in colors aglow.
Each story shared, a vibrant hue,
Together we craft, a world so true.

Through storms we stand, hand in hand,
In the fabric of time, we understand.
A tapestry rich, with love's embrace,
In every stitch, there's sacred space.

Moments captured, soft as a sigh,
In every loop, our spirits fly.
Echoes of joy, whispers of pain,
In the tapestry, all must remain.

Bound by the keep of cherished threads,
In the garden of hearts, our love spreads.
With every fold, and every crease,
In the tapestry of us, we find peace.

Curves of the Infinite Embrace

In the shadows where whispers play,
Curves entwine, night meets day.
Embracing soft, like ocean's tide,
In every arc, our joys confide.

With each embrace, the world dissolves,
In gentle arcs, our heart resolves.
Together we dance, in rhythms divine,
In curves of love, our souls align.

Boundless paths, we weave and trace,
In the depths of this warm space.
Every contour, a story told,
In the infinite, our hearts unfold.

Wrapped in warmth, the silence sings,
In the dance of time, eternity clings.
Curves of us, an endless chase,
In the fabric of life, we find our place.

The Language of Touch

Fingers brush, a soft refrain,
In silent words, love's sweet gain.
Every caress speaks volumes clear,
In this language, we draw near.

A gentle squeeze, a knowing glance,
In fleeting moments, hearts dance.
The warmth of skin, a tender breeze,
In every touch, our souls find ease.

Mapping paths where hearts collide,
In subtle gestures, we confide.
The world fades in a loving hush,
In the silence of touch, we rush.

So let our fingers weave and find,
The language of hearts, so intertwined.
In every moment, every hush,
In the essence of love, we trust.

Seasons of Tenderness

Spring whispers life, a gentle tease,
In every bloom, a song of ease.
Hearts awaken, in colors bright,
In the season of love, pure delight.

Summer's warmth, an endless day,
In golden rays, our worries stray.
With every laugh, joy intertwines,
In twinkling stars, our fate aligns.

Autumn leaves, a soft farewell,
In rustling whispers, secrets dwell.
With every drop, we hold so near,
In the twilight's glow, love perseveres.

Winter's chill, wrapped up close,
In cozy arms, we find our dose.
Through every season, come what may,
In tenderness shared, we'll always stay.

Once Upon a Moonlit Night

Beneath the glow of silver light,
The whispers of the night took flight.
Shadows dance on gentle streams,
As dreams unravel in moonlit beams.

A breeze that sings of tales untold,
Of lovers lost, and hearts of gold.
Each moment laced with tender grace,
A memory etched, a warm embrace.

The stars above, they brightly shine,
As secrets weave through space and time.
In solitude, the heart feels free,
As nature hums its lullaby's plea.

In this realm where whispers play,
The night unfolds its sweet ballet.
With every sigh, the night grows bold,
A story of love that never grows old.

Beneath the Symphony of Starlight

Under vastness, silence reigns,
A harmony that breaks all chains.
Stars like diamonds, bright and pure,
Illuminating dreams that endure.

The cosmos sings a haunting tune,
That echoes softly, like a boon.
In every glimmer, stories weave,
Of ancient souls who dared believe.

Hands entwined, we trace the sky,
With every wish, our spirits fly.
In the night's embrace, we find,
The melody of hearts combined.

Together lost in cosmic dance,
We twirl and spin in sweet romance.
The stars above bearing witness,
To love's eternal, boundless fitness.

A Voyage of Heartfelt Promises

Across the waves, we sail anew,
With hopes as vast as ocean blue.
Each promise made, a guiding star,
Leading us to where dreams are.

Through storms that rage and winds that howl,
Our hearts beat strong, we won't disavow.
Anchored deep in trust and grace,
We'll navigate this sacred space.

Every sunset paints the sky,
A testament, we dare to fly.
With every dawn, a chance to start,
Each wave a note in love's great art.

In this voyage, hand in hand,
We'll write our tale across the sand.
A journey filled with laughter, tears,
Together facing all our fears.

The Pathway Carved by Connection

Beneath the sky, a road unfolds,
A tapestry of stories told.
Each step we take, a bond refined,
In the embrace of the intertwined.

With every word, our hearts align,
In silent spaces, love will shine.
Together we walk, side by side,
In the warmth of trust, we confide.

The pathway glimmers, soft and bright,
Guided gently by shared light.
Every glance, a promise sworn,
In this journey, love is born.

Through every twist, through every turn,
In each connection, a passion burns.
Here, in the moment, we reside,
In the beauty of souls colliding.

The Dance of Celestial Flames

In the night, stars alight,
Whispers soft, a cosmic flight.
Fiery trails across the dark,
Each flicker tells a spark.

Galaxies twirl in a grand ballet,
Eternal beauty on display.
In the vastness, we find our place,
Lost in the dance, a fleeting grace.

Comets streak with tails of gold,
Stories of wonder yet untold.
Nebulae bloom like flowers rare,
Colorful dreams, without a care.

Embers glow, the universe sways,
Time dissolves in light's warm rays.
In this magic, we're never alone,
The celestial fires call us home.

In the Embrace of Forevermore

Wrapped in moments, soft and sweet,
Where time and hearts entwine and meet.
In whispered vows, like gentle streams,
We linger in the land of dreams.

The sun sets low, the moon ascends,
A promise made that never ends.
Hands held tight through stormy weather,
In every breath, we're bound together.

Stars bear witness to our song,
Melodies where we both belong.
Echoes of laughter fill the air,
In the embrace, we're free to dare.

With every sunset, love ignites,
In the tapestry of night's delights.
Together we'll endure and soar,
In the embrace of forevermore.

Heartbeats in Sync

In the quiet, our pulses play,
A rhythmic dance, night turns to day.
Beating softly, a steady song,
In this harmony, we belong.

Eyes meet in a shared glance,
Lost in the magic, we take a chance.
With every heartbeat, a sigh, a thrill,
Connected souls, a bond to fulfill.

Time fades as we hold each other tight,
Wrapped in the warmth of the fading light.
With every moment, our spirits blend,
In this cadence, a love that won't end.

Through life's rhythm, hand in hand,
Together we walk, united we stand.
Our heartbeats echo, a soothing link,
Perfectly matched, in sync, we think.

The Infinite Trail of Us

Paths woven on this earthly plane,
Steps intertwined in joy and pain.
Every journey, a tale to tell,
With you beside me, all is well.

The horizon stretches, vast and wide,
With you, my love, I'll always abide.
Through valleys low and mountains high,
Together we soar, reaching the sky.

In every shadow, a light will gleam,
In every moment, chase the dream.
Memories blossom like flowers in spring,
In the trail of us, joy we bring.

With every step, the bond grows strong,
In this journey, we both belong.
Forever onward, the stars above,
We write our story, a tale of love.

Reflections in the Window of Hearts

In the glass, secrets dance,
Shadows whisper gentle hints,
Beneath the light of dreams,
Echoes of love's sweet prints.

Time stands still, memories gleam,
Visions of what once was true,
In every glance, a wild scheme,
Hearts intertwine like morning dew.

Each moment captured in time,
Reflections of joy and pain,
A tapestry, so sublime,
In silence, love's song remains.

The window frames our shared fate,
Two souls wrapped in tender sighs,
In its depths, we contemplate,
Our truth beneath the wide skies.

The Dance of Two Souls

Underneath the starry skies,
Two souls move, a gentle sway,
With each step, love's sweet reprise,
In this moment, night turns to day.

Every twirl brings a soft glow,
In rhythm, hearts begin to soar,
Lost in the flow, feelings grow,
As whispers of love call for more.

The music plays, a timeless tune,
Fingers laced, they will not part,
Every note a soft commune,
In this dance, they share one heart.

Through shadows and shimmering light,
They weave magic with their grace,
In the stillness of the night,
Two souls find their sacred place.

Beneath the Moon's Gentle Watch

Silver light bathes the earth,
As dreams awaken in the night,
Underneath the moon's soft girth,
Whispers glide on wings of flight.

Imaginations set ablaze,
With every gleam, a story starts,
In moonlit realms, we spend our days,
Finding peace within our hearts.

The stars twinkle in playful mirth,
As secrets linger in the breeze,
Together we reclaim our worth,
Beneath the trees, among the leaves.

In this solace, hopes revive,
We drink the beauty's pure embrace,
Fueled by dreams, we come alive,
Beneath the moon, we find our place.

Embracing the Unknown

With open arms, we face the dark,
Venturing where shadows lie,
In the silence, we leave a mark,
Courage found in a soft sigh.

Winds of change call out our name,
A path untraveled, wild and free,
Through the fears, we spark the flame,
Finding strength in what will be.

Each step forward, a leap of faith,
Magic wanders just beyond sight,
In the chaos, no room for hate,
Heartbeats guide us through the night.

Together we dance with our dreams,
Embracing every twist and turn,
In the mystery, hope redeems,
As through the unknown, we now learn.

Navigating the Stars of Desire

In the night's embrace we wander,
Dreams beyond the cosmic sea.
Whispers of hope grow fonder,
As hearts drift in a silent plea.

Guided by the light we chase,
Every wish upon a star.
In this vast and endless space,
You're my compass, near or far.

With each heartbeat, we take flight,
Mapping constellations bright.
Together we will navigate,
Through the darkness, hand in hand.

In this universe of fire,
Love ignites the skies we see.
Boundless, fierce, our hearts conspire,
To chart the stars of you and me.

Through the Veil of Intimacy

In the quiet, secrets breathe,
A tapestry of whispered dreams.
Two souls entwined, we believe,
In the warmth of tender beams.

Eyes that speak without a sound,
Echoes of our shared embrace.
In this space, no walls abound,
As we dance in gentle grace.

Through the veil, our truths unfold,
Touching hearts, we find our way.
In the silence, stories told,
Love's soft sighs will always stay.

With each glance, a spark ignites,
Illuminating paths of trust.
In the depths of quiet nights,
With you, intimacy is a must.

Harmony in Distant Shores

Waves embrace the sandy coast,
In the rhythm, hearts align.
Across the seas, we dream the most,
Finding solace in the divine.

Each horizon tells a tale,
Of lovers lost and found again.
With every breeze, we set our sail,
To the music of the rain.

In the echoes, we hear our song,
Resonating far and wide.
Underneath the stars, so strong,
Together, we will ever glide.

Though distant shores may call our names,
Our harmony endures the test.
Love's sweet dance, it remains the same,
In every wave, we find our rest.

The Map of Kindred Spirits

Two hearts roam through valleys deep,
An atlas drawn by fate's design.
In laughter shared, we wake from sleep,
A friendship pure, a love divine.

Paths converge as stories weave,
Every glance tells tales anew.
In every moment, we believe,
The world expands when shared with you.

With compass hearts, we journey wide,
Tracing lines of joy and pain.
In the bond that we know ties,
Even storms cannot restrain.

Kindred spirits, hand in hand,
Navigating life's embrace.
In the vastness, we will stand,
Together, finding our true place.

Bohemian Trails of Belonging

In the whispers of the dawn, we roam,
Footprints soft on paths unknown.
Colors bleed in vibrant hues,
Where souls unite, and hearts peruse.

Underneath the azure skies,
Laughter echoes, free and wise.
Dreamers dance on dusty roads,
Together weaving life's true codes.

With each turn, a tale unfolds,
Stories shared, like treasures gold.
Wanderlust, a gentle guide,
Through nature's arms, we bide our stride.

In the twilight's soft embrace,
We find our home, our sacred space.
Belonging found in wild array,
Bohemian souls, we live, we play.

The Stories Written in the Sky

When twilight paints the world anew,
Stars ignite with dreams in view.
Constellations weave their lore,
Guiding hearts to distant shores.

Each shimmer holds a memory,
Of hopes and dreams, wild and free.
They whisper secrets of the night,
In silvered beams, a cosmic light.

The moon, a guardian of our fate,
Illuminates paths we await.
In cosmic dance, we find our way,
Through stories etched in skies of gray.

So raise your eyes to heavens wide,
Embrace the tales that stars provide.
For in the vast, infinite sea,
Are stories waiting to be free.

Through the Eye of the Heart

In stillness found, we dare to see,
The world reflected deep in thee.
Through valleys dark and mountains high,
The eye of the heart will never lie.

Gentle whispers guide our way,
In labyrinths where shadows play.
Each breath a note in life's sweet song,
Resonating, where we belong.

With open hearts, we weave our dreams,
A tapestry of hopes and schemes.
With every story shared, we mend,
Connections forged without an end.

Through the eye of love, we find,
The ties that bind, the paths entwined.
In every moment, truth will start,
Beneath the gaze of the open heart.

The Luminous Path We Forge

Beneath the stars, we take our stand,
Hand in hand, through shifting sand.
With every step we light the way,
A luminous path where dreams can stay.

In shadows long, we seek the glow,
Of kindness shared, a gentle flow.
Each act of love, a spark ignites,
In unity, we find our rights.

Through trials faced, we rise anew,
Together strong, like morning dew.
The road ahead may twist and wind,
But in each other, strength we find.

With radiant hearts, we face the dawn,
Creating beauty, forever drawn.
On this voyage, our spirits soar,
In the luminous path we forge once more.

Navigating the Rivers of Us

In the current of our dreams, we drift,
Through whispering streams where secrets shift.
Beneath the stars, our paths entwine,
Each ripple tells the tale that's mine.

Waves of laughter, echoes so sweet,
We paddle forth in sync, complete.
With every bend, new depths we find,
In the rivers of us, love is blind.

Through storms we sail, our hearts secure,
Navigating fears, our bond is pure.
Like starlit nights, our skies collide,
In every tide, we shall abide.

With the sunrise casting gold anew,
We embark on waves of love so true.
In the vast expanse, our souls align,
Forever drifting, you and I entwine.

The Twilight Between Two Souls

In the twilight glow, our shadows dance,
A fleeting moment, a silent chance.
Between the dusk and dawn's embrace,
We find our truths in time and space.

Whispers linger where silence prays,
In the cosmic pull of evening's haze.
Eyes meeting softly, hearts in still,
Breath held together, an unspoken thrill.

In this gentle hour where dreams are spun,
Two souls unite, yet we feel as one.
A canvas painted in hues of gold,
Where the stories of our love unfold.

As twilight wanes, the stars awake,
In that brief hour, we boldly take.
Hand in hand, through night's sweet toll,
We forge a path between our souls.

Chronicles of Intimate Journeys

In pages worn by time's embrace,
We ink our tales in sacred space.
Each journey penned, a story stacked,
In quiet corners where dreams unpacked.

The laughter shared, the tears we shed,
In chapters written, where love has led.
With every glance, the moments grow,
In intimate dance, together we flow.

From pages turned, we learn our fate,
In whispered words, we celebrate.
With every passage, a bridge we build,
In this rich archive, our souls are filled.

As memories bloom like flowers in spring,
In these chronicles, our hearts take wing.
In every line, the truth shines bright,
Guided together through dark and light.

The Wayward Compass of Togetherness

With a compass broken, we roam unbound,
In the wild of life, true love is found.
Through paths uncharted, we boldly stride,
Together at the world's uncertain tide.

In a dance of fate, we spin and sway,
Lost in the wilderness, come what may.
With every misstep, we learn to trust,
In the wayward paths, our spirits adjust.

Maps may fade, but our hearts remain,
In laughter's echo, in joy and pain.
For every detour, a lesson learned,
In the fire of passion, our hearts burned.

As stars align in the galaxy's embrace,
The wayward compass leads us to grace.
Through storms and calm, side by side,
In togetherness, our love won't hide.

Illuminated by Your Smile

In the glow of dawn, your smile gleams,
A beacon bright, fulfilling dreams.
With every glance, the shadows flee,
Your laughter dances, wild and free.

In twilight's hush, the stars align,
Your presence wraps this heart of mine.
The world fades out, just you and me,
In this warm light, we're meant to be.

Through fleeting hours, our spirits soar,
In every moment, I love you more.
Your smile, a spark, ignites the day,
In your embrace, I long to stay.

As sunsets paint the skies in gold,
Your gentle warmth, a love untold.
With every heartbeat, we transcend time,
Illuminated by your smile, so sublime.

A Symphony of Soulmates

In perfect harmony, we entwine,
Our hearts compose a song divine.
A melody that never fades,
In every note, true love cascades.

With gentle whispers, fate has sewn,
A tapestry where two have grown.
Through life's grand stage, we take our part,
The symphony of every heart.

Together we dance through storm and sun,
A rhythm echoed, two become one.
In verses shared, our spirits sing,
The sweetest song, forever spring.

As time unfolds, we'll play our tune,
In twilight's glow, beneath the moon.
In every heartbeat, in every smile,
A symphony of soulmates, timeless and worthwhile.

Beneath the Canopy of Dreams

Underneath the stars, we find our peace,
A canopy of dreams that will never cease.
In whispered secrets, the night unfolds,
With every story, our love retold.

The moonlight dances on your skin,
A gentle glow, where love begins.
In the quietude, our spirits soar,
With every heartbeat, we explore.

Among the shadows, magic stirs,
In every glance, the world blurs.
Together we wander, hand in hand,
Beneath the stars, in wonderland.

In dreams we paint our wildest fears,
In every joy, we splash the tears.
A canvas rich with vibrant hues,
Beneath the canopy, it's me and you.

Crossing Bridges of Emotion

Across the stream of feeling deep,
We build our bridges, strong and steep.
From joy to sorrow, we navigate,
With every step, we cultivate.

Together we face the ebb and flow,
In every challenge, our love will grow.
Through laughter shared and silent cries,
On bridges built, our spirit flies.

With trust as our guide, we journey far,
A compass true, our guiding star.
In every heartbeat, connections blend,
Crossing bridges, lover and friend.

Though storms may rage and shadows loom,
Together we rise, dispel the gloom.
With hands entwined, we brave this flight,
Crossing bridges, fueled by light.

Echoes of Our Enchanted Fortunes

In twilight's hush, we weave our dreams,
With whispered hopes and starlit gleams.
Each heartbeat sings a tale so bright,
In the dance of shadows, we find our light.

The winds carry secrets of love untold,
In the pockets of time, our memories hold.
Through valleys deep and mountains high,
Together we stand, like the endless sky.

Beneath the moon's gentle, silvery gaze,
We trace the paths of our cherished days.
With laughter woven in every sigh,
In the tapestry of life, you and I.

So here we dwell in this sacred space,
Where echoes of fortune leave their trace.
In the magic spun by fate's own thread,
We find our way, where hearts are led.

The Chronicles of Kindred Spirits

In quiet corners, our stories blend,
Two souls entwined, as time transcends.
With every glance, a chapter unfolds,
In the warmth of friendship, our truth beholds.

Through storms we've weathered, hand in hand,
In laughter and tears, we take a stand.
Each moment cherished, a treasure found,
In the symphony of life, our hearts resound.

The pages turn with the seasons' grace,
In each embrace, I find my place.
With bonds unbroken, our spirits soar,
In the chronicles of love, we seek for more.

So let us write with ink of gold,
In the annals of time, our tales are told.
With every heartbeat, we'll craft our fate,
As kindred spirits, it's never too late.

The Garden Where We Bloom

In sunlight's kiss, our petals gleam,
In the garden of dreams, we find our theme.
With colors bright, we paint the sky,
Each blossom whispers, never goodbye.

The fragrance lingers in the morning light,
As roots entwine, we grow in might.
With every season, our love takes flight,
In the tender embrace of day and night.

We cultivate hope in the soil of care,
With gentle hands, our hearts laid bare.
In laughter's breeze, our spirits sway,
In the garden where love leads the way.

So let us nurture this sacred space,
With every heartbeat, we find our grace.
In the dance of blooms, forever we'll stay,
In the garden of life, come what may.

A Journey of Heartfelt Seasons

Through autumn's glow, our paths align,
Where harvest whispers, hearts entwine.
With winter's chill, we draw so near,
In the warmth of love, we cast out fear.

In spring's embrace, new life appears,
With every blossom, we shed our tears.
Through summer's laughter, we chase the sun,
In this journey of seasons, we are one.

With memories woven in threads of gold,
In every glance, our stories unfold.
Through time's embrace, we rise and fall,
In the rhythm of life, we hear love's call.

So hand in hand, let's wander wide,
In the seasons' dance, there's nothing to hide.
With every heartbeat, we find our way,
In this journey of love, come what may.

Threads of Connection

In whispers soft, we weave our dreams,
Through laughter's light, or silent gleams.
A tapestry of moments shared,
In every thread, our hearts laid bare.

With gentle pulls, we find our way,
In colors bright, both night and day.
Each knot tied firm, a bond so true,
In every stitch, I am with you.

Through storms we face, our strength will show,
In shadows cast, our love will grow.
Together here, we stand, we bind,
In threads of gold, two souls aligned.

As seasons change, our fabric flows,
In patterns rich, our journey shows.
With every twist, our stories blend,
In this shared weave, we transcend.

Undercurrents of Devotion

Beneath the surface, love does flow,
In currents deep, where feelings grow.
Unseen by most, yet felt so clear,
In every heartbeat, I hold you near.

When silence speaks, our spirits dance,
In fleeting glances, there's a chance.
The ties that bind, though often hidden,
In whispered vows, our lives are woven.

Through tempests wild, our compass stays,
In gentle tides, we find our ways.
The depths we reach, the warmth we find,
In undercurrents, our souls aligned.

For in the quiet, truths unfold,
In sacred depths, our stories told.
Embracing all that we can't see,
In currents vast, it's you and me.

Footprints in Shared Silence

In quiet moments, we both stand,
With whispers soft, a gentle hand.
Footprints etched in sand and stone,
A silent pact, we are not alone.

In every pause, our hearts converse,
In stillness deep, we share our verse.
Together here, in silence sweet,
A language forged, where souls entreat.

As twilight falls, our shadows merge,
In tranquil sights, our spirits surge.
A testament to all we've shared,
In footprints laid, our love is bared.

When echoes fade, and stars align,
In this soft hush, your heart is mine.
With every step, together stride,
In shared silence, love won't hide.

The Road Less Traveled Together

On winding paths, we take our chance,
With every step, a sweet romance.
The road less traveled, rough and true,
I find my way, when I'm with you.

Through bramble thorns and skies of gray,
In moments dim, you light my way.
Side by side, our fears we meet,
In all the trials, love feels complete.

With laughter bright, we chase the dawn,
In every battle, our strength reborn.
Far from the norm, we carve our trail,
In shared adventures, we shall not fail.

Each mile we roam, a story told,
In every turn, our hearts unfold.
Together bound, in joy we tether,
This journey shared, our lives together.

The Silent Language of Souls

In whispers soft, we weave our ties,
A glance can speak where silence lies.
Our hearts converse in subtle grace,
In every moment, your soul I trace.

With every sigh, a story shown,
In quiet depths, we've both grown.
No need for words, just trust the feel,
In hushed embrace, our bonds reveal.

The echoes of a love unspoke,
In tranquil dreams, our fates provoke.
In shadows cast, our spirits dance,
A symphony of the heart's romance.

As twilight's glow begins to fade,
In silent vows, the night won't trade.
We breathe in sync, the world our stage,
In this stillness, we turn the page.

Through Twists of Fate We Wander

Down winding paths, we find our way,
Through stormy nights and bright sunny days.
With every step, the road unfolds,
A tapestry of tales retold.

In serendipity, our hearts collide,
With open arms, we drift and glide.
Through twists of fate, a dance we share,
In life's embrace, we cast our care.

The compass guides but veers us near,
With trust, we walk, dispelling fear.
Each choice we make, a thread we weave,
In the journey's heart, we dare believe.

Together here, through trials and cheer,
The stars align, our purpose clear.
With every moment, a spark ignites,
In love's embrace, our souls take flight.

The Shadows and Lights of Us

In shadows deep, our secrets play,
With glimmers bright, they light the way.
We dance between the dark and glow,
In every moment, our spirits flow.

The laughter sings, the tears may fall,
In every rise, we heed the call.
Together strong, we face the night,
In unity, we find our light.

Reflecting truths in love's warm hue,
With every clash, we start anew.
The storm may rage, yet still we stand,
In each other's hearts, we find our land.

Through every shade, our colors blend,
In shadows cast, our stories mend.
And as we shine, the world will see,
The beauty born of you and me.

Guided by the North Star of Affection

In silent nights, where dreams converge,
We find the truth, where feelings surge.
The North Star shines, a guide so bright,
Illuminating paths of love and light.

With every turn, our hearts align,
In gentle whispers, your hand in mine.
Through winding roads, we chart our course,
In love's embrace, we find our force.

With open hearts, we navigate,
Through storms and calm, we trust our fate.
The guide above, our faithful spark,
In every journey, we leave our mark.

Together here, forever bound,
In every heartbeat, solace found.
As starlit skies blanket the night,
Guided by love, we take our flight.

Beneath the Arbor of Dreams

In the shade of ancient trees,
Whispers dance with summer breeze.
Colors blend in twilight's gleam,
Hearts unite, beneath the dream.

Stars awaken, dim and bright,
Casting hopes into the night.
Every sigh, a secret shared,
In this haven, souls are bared.

Crickets sing, a gentle sound,
Courage blooms upon the ground.
Laughter rings, shadows flicker,
Moments pause, the clock runs quicker.

Beneath the boughs, we find our place,
Time surrenders, lost in grace.
Together, weaving tales anew,
Beneath the dreams, just me and you.

Steps Beside the Flowing Stream

Gentle ripples, soft and clear,
Guide our thoughts as we draw near.
Each step echoes nature's song,
Together here, we both belong.

Pebbles glint in sunlit rays,
Whispers weave through tranquil days.
Footprints mark the path we've tread,
Memories linger, never dead.

Mossy banks where wildflowers bloom,
Sharing dreams, dispelling gloom.
Every glance, a silent plea,
Steps beside this flowing sea.

Time unwinds like distant chime,
Held in rhythm, love in rhyme.
Hand in hand, we drift as one,
Beneath the sky, our hearts are spun.

The Map of Shared Sentiment

Lines and curves draw paths unknown,
Across the world we can't postpone.
Every mark a story traced,
In whispered dreams, our hopes are placed.

Moments gathered, memories wide,
Charting journeys, hearts as guide.
Ink of love on parchment strewn,
Guiding light beneath the moon.

Every tear and every laugh,
Sketches fill this simple craft.
With each step, our spirits soar,
Together tracing evermore.

In the folds, our destinies lie,
Beyond the hills, beneath the sky.
A tapestry of ties that bind,
In this map, our lives aligned.

Embracing the Journey Together

Wheels turn on this winding road,
With every mile, our bond is showed.
Hand in hand, we face the skies,
In each challenge, our spirits rise.

Moments fleeting, yet they stay,
In laughter's glow, we find our way.
Through the storms and sunny days,
Together, love finds its ways.

Voices blend in harmony,
Finding strength in you and me.
With dreams alight, we'll brave the test,
Embracing all that we know best.

Endless horizons call our name,
In this journey, nothing's the same.
Hand in hand, with hearts aglow,
Together onward, ever we go.

Pathways of Silent Promises

In the quiet of the night,
We wander side by side,
Footsteps softly intertwine,
Where secrets dare to hide.

With each promise softly spoken,
Hearts beat in a gentle rhyme,
Pathways made from whispered words,
In the fabric of our time.

Stars above shine bright for us,
Guiding through the endless dark,
In this vast and open world,
Your love ignites a spark.

Silent vows, like shadows cast,
Walk with me this sacred road,
Together we will forge ahead,
With every heavy load.

Blossom Between Us

Petals fall like gentle whispers,
In the garden where we meet,
Colors blend with soft embraces,
Nature's rhythm guides our beat.

Sunlight dances on our skin,
As we weave a tale anew,
Moments linger, sweetly shared,
In the bloom of morning dew.

Raindrops kiss the earth below,
As our laughter fills the air,
Every blossom tells a story,
Of a bond beyond compare.

In the fragrance of together,
Every heartbeat sings so free,
Growing stronger, side by side,
In a love that's meant to be.

Trails Woven in Trust

Beneath the canopy of trees,
We march along the winding way,
Every step, a leap of faith,
In trust, we choose to stay.

With eyes that spark like distant stars,
Guiding through the thickened mist,
Every echo of our laughter,
A testament of all we've missed.

Paths diverge but hearts align,
In this dance of give and take,
Through the hurdles, we will rise,
For each other's sake.

In the silence, bonds grow strong,
With whispers of our shared dreams,
Together, we will navigate,
The flow of life's wild streams.

The Palette of Shared Moments

In the hues of fading light,
We gather shades of memories,
Brushstrokes bright upon the canvas,
Painting life with reveries.

A splash of laughter here and there,
Emotions rich and deep indeed,
Each moment crafted with such care,
In our hearts, the colors lead.

From soft pastels to vibrant tints,
Every heartbeat finds its place,
Together, we create a world,
Filled with love and warm embrace.

With every stroke, a story told,
In the gallery of our days,
The palette glows with shared delight,
In countless, wondrous ways.

The Reservoir of Unspoken Promises

In shadows deep, beneath the skies,
Whispers dance where silence lies.
A river flows of dreams untold,
Where secrets bloom, and hearts unfold.

Upon the banks where hopes entwine,
Each sigh a pledge, a sacred line.
We tread the paths of gentle grace,
In this reserve, our souls embrace.

Time stands still, as visions blend,
In quiet moments, we can mend.
The weight of words that fade away,
Yet linger still, in soft array.

Through twilight's veil, we softly roam,
In unspoken vows, we've found our home.
A reservoir where trust descends,
Eternity's breath as love transcends.

Winding Through a Meadow of Hearts

Beneath the sun, where shadows play,
We wander through the bright array.
Each flower sways with whispers sweet,
As love blooms softly at our feet.

The gentle breeze, a tender guide,
In every glance, we feel our pride.
The laughter twirls like leaves in air,
In this meadow, hearts lay bare.

Each step we take, a song is sung,
The melodies of youth still young.
In golden light, our spirits rise,
As dreams take flight beneath blue skies.

Together we weave a tapestry,
Of moments shared, just you and me.
In this haven, forever stay,
In winding paths, we find our way.

On the Ribbon of Time Together

Time unravels like a gentle thread,
We stitch our dreams where lovers tread.
Each day a stitch, so firm and kind,
On ribbons lost, our hearts aligned.

Through seasons worn, we weave our tale,
In laughter's echo, we prevail.
The moments shared, both sweet and rare,
Are threads of love beyond compare.

With every laugh, each sigh, each tear,
The fabric of our bond grows near.
Wrapped in warmth, in twilight's glow,
On ribbons of time, our souls bestow.

Forever woven, hand in hand,
In this tapestry, we understand.
For every stitch, our love reclaims,
A ribbon danced in endless flames.

The Seasons of Passionate Paths

The springtime blooms with colors bright,
Awakens hearts to pure delight.
In summer's warmth, our laughter flows,
As passion's fire forever grows.

With autumn's chill, we feel the gleam,
Of dreams fulfilled, and love supreme.
As leaves fall down, we hold them tight,
In fleeting moments, pure and bright.

When winter comes, the nights are long,
Yet in the silence, we stay strong.
With every snowfall, hearts ignite,
In cozy dreams, we find the light.

Through every season, hand in hand,
We journey forth, a steadfast band.
In pathways forged by love's embrace,
The seasons change, but we find grace.

Blossoms on the Road to Us

Along the winding path we tread,
Colors dance beneath our feet.
Whispers of joy softly spread,
Every moment is a sweet treat.

In spring's embrace, our hearts align,
Petals falling like gentle rain.
Hand in hand, we feel divine,
Each step taken eases pain.

Sunlight filters through the trees,
Casting shadows long and bright.
With laughter carried by the breeze,
We weave love's tapestry of light.

As blossoms bloom, our spirits soar,
With every turn, new dreams arise.
Together we'll explore and more,
In this journey, love never dies.

Through the Storms of the Heart

When thunder rumbles in the night,
And shadows loom with heavy dread,
We hold each other, hearts alight,
Finding strength when hope has fled.

The rain may fall with fierce despair,
Yet warm embraces chase the chill.
We'll navigate this tempest's snare,
Trusting love's unwavering will.

In the eye of the storm, we pause,
Feeling calm amidst the strife.
A quiet moment, no applause,
Just us together, bound in life.

As clouds disperse and sunlight gleams,
We rise above what tried to part.
In every challenge, grow our dreams,
Together, through the storms of heart.

Illuminated Paths of Togetherness

Stars ignite the darkened skies,
Guiding us with gentle light.
In your gaze, I see the prize,
With you, the world feels just right.

Each step we take, the glow expands,
Shadows fade where love ignites.
With open hearts, we join our hands,
Creating magic, reaching heights.

Through dusk and dawn, our spirits blend,
Woven threads of fate and trust.
In every moment, we transcend,
A bond that's destined, pure, and just.

So let us wander, side by side,
On these illuminated ways.
In each other, we confide,
Together, we ignite our days.

The Canvas of Our Sweet Journey

With colors bright, our story's told,
Each brushstroke sings a melody.
In every shade, our love unfolds,
A vibrant dance of destiny.

Moments captured, laughter shared,
On this canvas, heartbeats blend.
With every hue, our hearts declared,
This journey, love will always send.

From gentle pastels to bold strokes,
We paint our dreams in twilight's glow.
In every detail, laughter stokes,
This masterpiece, a cherished flow.

As we create, time drifts away,
Yet here we stay, with hearts aglow.
Together, come what may,
In the canvas of our sweet journey, we'll grow.

www.ingramcontent.com/pod-product-compliance
Ingram Content Group UK Ltd.
Pitfield, Milton Keynes, MK11 3LW, UK
UKHW021655281224
452765UK00007B/77